AI in Politics

Election Forecasting, Campaign Strategies, and Governance

Table of Contents

Chapter 1. Introduction

Welcome to our comprehensive Special Report that dives into the fascinating intersection of Artificial Intelligence (AI) and Politics. As technology evolves, it continues to mold various aspects of our daily lives, notably, the political landscape is not left untouched. In this report, we delve into its profound impact on election forecasting, campaign strategies, and governance. While the topic may seem advanced and complex, we assure you - there's no need for a computer science degree to appreciate the transformation at hand! Written in an accessible and clear style, this report demystifies AI's influence in politics and offers keen insights into the shifting dynamics. Brace yourself for an illuminating journey that explores the future of politics as directed by the invisible yet influential hand of AI. Trust us, it's a page-turner you wouldn't want to miss!

Chapter 2. The Convergence of AI and Politics: An Introduction

Artificial Intelligence (AI), a term coined in 1956 by John McCarthy, stands at the technological forefront, promising to revolutionize various sectors of society. Politics, a domain integral to any society's functioning, is no exception to this transformation. The convergence of AI and politics, an intersection as enigmatic as it is profound, presents an exciting new pathway for study and exploration.

2.1. Understanding Artificial Intelligence

At its core, AI refers to machine or computer programs capable of performing tasks that often require human intelligence, thanks to their ability to learn and apply knowledge. But the concept doesn't stop with just task execution. Modern AI includes systems that can learn, reason, and improve over time, making them integral tools in predicting phenomena, understanding complex concepts, and solving problems that humans alone might find difficult.

In recent years, AI's development has been dramatic, moving from the realm of science fiction into everyday reality. This rapid advancement is due to breakthroughs in Machine Learning (ML) - an application of AI - that provides systems the ability to learn and improve from experience. Particularly, Deep Learning, a subset of Machine Learning, has made it possible for AI to process enormous data sets and effectively make predictions or decisions without the aid of explicit programming.

AI is everywhere around us – from voice assistants and personalized algorithms to automated customer service and self-driving cars – transforming industries and social landscapes.

2.2. AI Meets Politics

As pervasive as it is transformative, AI's influence has inevitably reached the realm of politics. In its broadest sense, politics is about individuals and groups making collective decisions. Information, persuasion, communication, and strategic decision-making are all vital elements within this sphere. With the unique capabilities AI offers, it's not hard to see why the idea of intertwined AI and politics is quickly gaining traction.

AI's impact on politics can be observed in three broad areas: election forecasting, campaign strategies, and governance. First, AI algorithms can analyze large quantities of data to predict election outcomes, providing valuable insights for campaign strategies. Second, AI can help personalize political messages, increasing their effectiveness and resonance with voters. Lastly, in the area of governance, AI can shape public policy making, optimize public service delivery, and even assist in law enforcement.

Moreover, AI's influence is not confined to these measurable impacts alone. It is increasingly influencing political discourse, driving conversations about regulation and ethical considerations surrounding its use.

2.3. AI and Election Forecasting

With the advent of Big Data, vast amounts of data related to the electorate are becoming available – from social media posts to details of previous voting behavior. This data, when analyzed by AI algorithms, can provide invaluable insights that could potentially predict election outcomes.

Several election prediction models are based on machine-learning algorithms, which improve their accuracy over time as they learn from more and more data. Apart from voting data, these algorithms can analyze public sentiment on social media and political forums, economic indicators, demographic information, and more - creating a detailed picture of the political landscape that can engineer highly accurate predictions.

2.4. AI and Campaign Strategies

AI's influence extends to campaign strategies, where it helps political parties and candidates reach voters more effectively. A prime example of this is 'microtargeting,' a practice that employs AI to deliver personalized messages to specific segments of the electorate based on their likeliness to respond positively. Microtargeting involves analyzing vast amounts of data to gain insights about individual voters' preferences and behaviors, and these insights can be used to tailor political messages that resonate more strongly.

Also, AI can be used to analyze the impact and performance of different campaign elements. Using AI, campaign managers can easily adjust their strategies on the fly, adapting messages, mediums, and man-hours based on real-time feedback.

2.5. AI in Governance

Beyond elections, AI has substantial implications for governance. For example, data-driven decision making in public policy can benefit from AI's predictive capabilities. Machine learning algorithms can analyze trends and patterns in large datasets, providing valuable evidence to inform the creation and implementation of public policies.

In public service delivery, AI can streamline operations and improve efficiency. From optimizing traffic management to increasing the speed of processing paperwork, AI can make government services more effective and user-friendly. Additionally, AI's potential to assist in law enforcement can significantly enhance areas like cybersecurity, crime prediction, and surveillance.

At a broader level, AI can enable more direct and participatory forms of democracy. Through AI-powered political bots, governments could potentially interact with citizens in a more personalized manner, receiving feedback, suggestions, and grievances directly from each individual and addressing them in real-time.

The potential of AI in politics is far from fully realized. Ensuring the responsible and ethical use of AI technologies in the political landscape is vital. The growing impact of AI in shaping democracies across the world necessitates a broad discourse on its potential benefits and challenges. Vigilance is crucial to ensure we take full advantage of what AI has in store for politics, without compromising the values and integrity upon which our societies are built. Yet, with conscientious use and diligent oversight, the convergence of AI and politics could mark a novel chapter in the annals of democratic governance.

Chapter 3. Election Forecasting: AI's Crystal Ball

Predicting the outcome of elections has been a focus of political science for years, a crystal ball as it were, to gauge the ebb and flow of our democratic processes. Over time these predictions have become more sophisticated, moving from the poll-based methodologies of yesterday to today's data-driven models. A significant enabler in this leap has been the advent and adoption of artificial intelligence (AI).

3.1. The Birth of Election Forecasting with AI

The roots of artificial intelligence in election forecasting can be traced back to the early years of the 21st century when statisticians began using machine learning algorithms to predict election outcomes. These predictive models utilized voter data, along with demographic, economic, and geopolitical variables to train and test machine learning models. This era saw a shift in the paradigm with the focus moving from voter sentiments, which was subjective, to a more empirical and analytical model.

AI algorithms digest massive amounts of data, identify patterns, learn from past mistakes, and make increasingly accurate predictions. Machine learning, a subset of AI, focuses on using algorithms to parse data, learn from it, and then apply learning to make deterministic predictions or decisions.

The first significant indicator of AI-powered election forecasting was in the 2012 U.S. Presidential Election when "Polls-Plus" forecast created by Nate Silver's FiveThirtyEight accurately predicted the outcome of the election in all 50 states.

3.2. Unpacking the Process: AI in Election Forecasting

At the heart of it, election forecasting models built utilizing AI use regression and classification algorithms, along with novel techniques like natural language processing (NLP) to analyze and predict election results.

Regression algorithms are utilized to predict how much of the vote each candidate might win in a specific geographical area. Regression algorithms take into account features like political leaning of the area, previous voting patterns, demographic data, economic indicators and more.

Classification algorithms, on the other hand, help us understand if a candidate will win or lose in a certain district or state. These algorithms take into consideration similar data points as regression models but provide outputs as win/lose classification instead of vote proportions.

Natural language processing techniques enable AI to analyze public opinion, sentiment, and topical discussions on social media platforms.

It's essential to note that AI election forecasting models require robust, accurate, and unbiased data. The more comprehensive and precise the data, the more accurate the forecast.

3.3. Innovations and Breakthroughs: AI Takes the Stage

As AI's availability and sophistication have grown, we've witnessed transformative breakthroughs in the field of election forecasting. For instance, in 2016, MogIA, an AI system developed by an Indian startup accurately predicted Donald Trump's victory, based on 20 million data points from public platforms, which demonstrated AI's potential to gauge public sentiment effectively.

Further advancements in AI, specifically in the area of deep learning, have allowed for real-time sentiment analysis by sifting through millions of social media posts and online discussions. The rise of deep learning has increased forecasting model accuracy by managing complex and large datasets, thereby producing highly accurate predictions.

3.4. The Challenges Ahead: AI in Election Forecasting

Despite AI's promise, challenges remain. Data bias is a significant concern, with algorithms only being as good as the data they're being fed. Inaccurate, incomplete, or skewed data can lead to incorrect predictions.

Another challenge is the black-box nature of certain AI methodologies, particularly deep-learning models. The lack of transparency and interpretability in these methods can lead to unwarranted trust in their predictions without understanding the underlying assumptions or logic.

Lastly, despite AI's potential in predicting outcomes, it does not replace the need for human interpretation and understanding of the political landscape. Experts must contextualize the AI's prediction within the broader geopolitical, economic, and societal landscape.

3.5. Towards the Future: AI and Election Forecasting

AI continues to evolve and become more deeply integrated into every aspect of our lives. As such, it is only natural that AI's role in election forecasting will continue to increase.

With advancements in AI, we may see more personalized election prediction models developed, where voters have personalized predictions based on their individual data. While this may raise privacy concerns, with appropriate safeguards, it could revolutionize how we engage with our democratic processes.

Additionally, advances in AI transparency and interpretability are just around the corner, helping us trust the predictions of AI even more. Interpretability will also allow for improved accuracies, as experts will be able to tweak models based on political intuition and nuances.

AI in election forecasting is here to stay. Not only will it continue to make predictions more accurate, but it may also change how we engage with politics, encouraging a more data-driven approach to understanding and participating in our democratic processes. The crystal ball of politics is looking increasingly digital and AI-powered, shining light on the road ahead like never before.

Chapter 4. AI in Tailoring Innovative Campaign Strategies

In the world of political campaigning, the goal has always been clear: to connect with voters in meaningful ways that inspire action. For decades, this meant relying on traditional modes of communication such as door-knocking, leaflets, televised ads, and speeches. Today, however, the advent of AI technology has radically reshaped the landscape of political campaign strategies, making it possible to engage with voters on an unprecedented scale and with a level of personalization that was once unimaginable.

4.1. The Dawn of Data in Political Campaigns

Arguably, the largest impact AI has made on campaign strategies centers on the increasingly sophisticated use of data. Gone are the days when a candidate's breadth of support could be gauged through a cheering crowd at a rally or the number of yard signs splayed across the neighborhood. The proliferation of online platforms today allows for a wealth of data to be harvested, analyzed, and utilized in more strategic ways.

It begins with data collection. During a political campaign, every interaction made online by voters is a reservoir of potentially useful information. Through website analytics, social media interactions, or even AI-managed communications such as chatbots, data on voter preferences, key issues they care about, and their sentiment towards a candidate can be scooped and streamlined into a data bank.

From here, AI steps in to mine and analyze this data in real-time.

Machine learning algorithms, a subfield of AI, can process and interpret vast amounts of information in ways that were beyond the scope of manual data analysts. These algorithms can extract patterns, predict voter behavior, and even prescribe tailored messaging aimed at swaying undecided voters, all the while constantly learning and refining their predictions.

4.2. Microtargeting: The Art of Personalized Politics

From this pool of analyzed data springs the new-age campaign strategy: Microtargeting. This approach takes the data-driven insights about a person, their preferences, hopes, and fears, and leverages them to curate personalized messages that resonate deeply. Political campaigns can use algorithms to create voter profiles, segmenting them based on demographics, political leanings, and even psychographics.

These highly-specific voter segments can then be targeted with tailored messages across different communication platforms. For example, advertisements or campaign messages on social media platforms can focus on issues relevant to a particular segment. AI can even optimize the timing and format of these messages to ensure they capture the user's attention.

Beyond just messaging, this customized campaign approach can be harnessed in volunteer and get-out-the-vote efforts. By predicting which voters are likely to support a candidate but may not turn out, AI algorithms can help campaigns target their resources effectively, whether that's in offering rides to the polls or sending reminders on Election Day.

4.3. Predictive Analytics in Campaign Strategy

Predictive analytics is another powerful tool born from the marriage of AI and campaign strategizing. AI systems, armed with historical data, societal trends, and real-time polling numbers, can help forecast election outcomes with greater accuracy than traditional polling methods. More importantly, they can draw insights that help campaigns adjust their strategies.

By following how voter sentiment fluctuates in response to particular events or messages, campaigns can optimize their strategies and messaging in real time. Consider a situation in which certain policy proposals are witnessing a surge in online discussions. Predictive analytics would highlight this, and the candidate could capitalize on the engaged audience by promptly addressing related issues.

Predictive analytics can also inform campaigns where their candidates may be faring poorly and need to focus more resources. These insights are game-changing, allowing campaigns to adapt and respond quickly to the changing political landscape.

4.4. Ethics and Limitations in AI-led Campaigning

Just as AI has opened paradigm-shifting possibilities in election campaigning, it has also ushered in complex ethical concerns. Chief among them is the issue of privacy. The microtargeting strategy relies on gathering personal information, raising questions about consent, cyber security, and the potential abuse of personal data.

Further, unregulated use of AI in campaigning can foster misinformation or disinformation. Personalized messages, when misused, can become vehicles for manipulation, distorting a voter's understanding of a candidate or issue.

Moreover, algorithms could unintentionally amplify existing biases if they are trained solely on past data. For instance, a system may wrongly predict a low turnout in areas with historically low engagement, influencing how resources are allocated and potentially perpetuating the low turnout cycle.

4.5. The Future is AI: Gazing into the Crystal Ball

In the grand scheme of things, we're at the cusp of the AI revolution in political campaigning. Despite its challenges and limitations, AI holds astounding potential for elevating the democratic process. As understanding of the technology develops and regulations are established, AI can make political campaigns more personalized, efficient, and potentially more transparent.

Looking forward, we can envision AI increasingly integrated within the fabric of campaign campaigning. From AI-managed town halls and debates to machine learning-enhanced policy development, the role of this technology is set to grow. This denotes a future where the dichotomy between voters and politicians shrinks, and a political landscape that is more inclusive, fluid, and representative takes shape.

However, for all these promising transformations, it is crucial to steer this technology in a direction that prioritizes democracy, transparency, and the voter's agency. AI's unstoppable march into the realm of politics presents an unambiguous call for thoughtful engagement, advanced understanding, and ethical considerations. To harness its potential responsibly and effectively, politicians, campaigners, and the public alike will need to navigate this evolving territory with care, rigour, and ultimately a knowledge-driven approach.

Chapter 5. AI and Governance: Effective Policy Making or Ethical Dilemma?

In the landscape of governance and policy-making, the pivotal role of information cannot be understated. As the fuel of modern decision-making, possessing timely and accurate information is essential. The rise of artificial intelligence (AI) promises to revamp policy-making with its ability to gather, analyze and interpret massive data swiftly. Yet, it introduces new ethical dilemmas on a scale we have never encountered before.

5.1. The AI Influence on Policy Making

The objective of policy making is primarily to address societal issues. Policy designs aim to be informed, evidence-based choices that best serve its people and environment. Here, AI's data-driven decision-making capabilities can be invaluable. Through AI's predictive analysis, policy-makers can anticipate consequences and make viable decisions. It removes the guesswork, instead proffering concrete evidence-based policies.

For instance, AI has been utilized in policy-making related to climate change. Complex algorithms analyze vast environmental data, providing reliable predictions on climate trends. This information allows governments to draft policies that address projected concerns efficiently.

Similarly, AI analytics has been applied in urban planning and health policies. AI-driven predictive policing strategies have also been adopted in several cities, using pattern recognition to manage crime.

These examples demonstrate how AI can empower governments to make informed decisions, enhance governance and improve citizens' wellbeing.

5.2. The Risks: AI's Ethical Dilemmas

Despite the profound potential benefits, AI's intersection with politics is fraught with ethical complexities. Chief among these is the issue about transparency and accountability.

AI systems often function on opaque "black box" models. As these models are complex, the decision-making process behind AI's recommendations remains largely unknown. This conundrum known as the "black box" problem poses a serious challenge to a democratic society that values transparency in decision-making.

The use of predictive policing strategies reveals an example. These AI systems rely on historical crime data. Yet this data may carry inherent biases, reflecting years of systemic bias in law enforcement. The AI, in this case, is not neutral but may perpetuate patterns of discrimination, problematically encoding bias into future police activity.

5.3. AI Regulation: Balancing Innovation and Protection

The confluence of AI and politics necessitates regulatory measures to keep the technology in check. However, the dynamic nature of AI presents challenges for classic regulatory approaches. As the technology evolves rapidly, laws can't seem to catch up.

The current conversation around AI regulation hinges on drawing lines between fostering innovation and ensuring protection. Heavy regulations can stifle technological advancement, while light regulations may not protect against misuse of AI. This conundrum calls for a delicate balancing act that is yet to be perfected.

A prominent example of governmental attempts at regulating AI is the European Union's General Data Protection Regulation (GDPR). It is considered one of the broadest and most comprehensive data privacy laws in the world. While predominantly focused on data privacy, it also includes provisions on algorithms and AI, such as a user's right to explanation when an automated decision has been made.

5.4. Towards AI-Driven Governance: The Road Ahead

It's clear that AI stands to revolutionize governance. But equally, it raises ethical and regulatory challenges that we've yet to solve. As we forge ahead, democratic values of transparency, accountability, and fairness must continue to guide our navigation of these uncharted waters.

Indeed, the narrative of AI and governance is far from complete and continues to evolve. Crucially, it is our awareness, vigilance, and adaptability that will determine the success of this AI-driven transformation.

The intersection of AI and governance is both exciting and fraught with challenges. If harnessed properly, AI could empower governance to make proactive, informed policies, foster innovation, and enrich societal values. The ethical and regulatory dilemmas it brings, however, also necessitate robust discussions and thoughtful legislative actions.

In conclusion, the potential for AI to improve governance is immense, but the road to effective and ethical AI-driven policy-making requires careful navigation. As AI continues to transform the political landscape, responsible leadership and informed citizenry shall be the anchor guiding us through the tides of this transition.

Chapter 6. Navigating through Data: AI's Role in Voter Profiling

Data has become the lifeblood of politics in the modern era. And at the very heart of political data sit the voters, the constituents, who hold the power to decide who leads, who influences policy, and the overall direction of governance. This is where artificial intelligence (AI) proves pivotal—offering sophisticated tools for voter profiling, which involves collecting data about voters and making projections about their behavior.

6.1. Understanding Voter Profiling

Voter profiling is the process of compiling individual voter data—ranging from demographic details and political affiliations to consumer behavior—to develop a comprehensive picture of voting patterns and trends. In the past, this involved a great deal of manual labor, and the profiles created were often imprecise and generalized. But with the development of AI, the process has become far more accurate and personalized.

AI fuels what we call predictive modeling, a scientific methodology that uses statistics and data management to forecast outcomes. In voter profiling, AI algorithms gather data from various sources, determine patterns in the data, and create predictive models on voter behavior. These models allow politicians and policy-makers to target specific demographics more effectively, crafting messages that speak to particular voters' political needs and concerns.

6.2. The Nuts and Bolts: AI in Action

The application of AI in voter profiling involves several steps, each making use of different AI technologies. These steps range from data gathering and sorting to pattern recognition and predictive modeling.

One of the main tools used in these steps is machine learning (ML), a subset of AI that enables systems to learn from data, identify patterns, and make decisions without being explicitly programmed. By using ML algorithms, large volumes of data can be processed and grouped together in a fraction of the time it would take a team of data scientists.

In the voter profiling context, ML enables the creation of individual voter profiles by analyzing historical voting data, social media activity, survey responses, and other information sources. This information is then synthesized and patterns identified, allowing for the prediction of future voting behavior.

Another key AI technology used in voter profiling is natural language processing (NLP). NLP enables computer systems to understand human language in a useful and meaningful way. In voter profiling, this technology is often applied in analyzing social media posts, gauging public sentiment, and identifying issues that resonate with voters.

The predictive models generated by ML and NLP are instrumental in carving out personalized campaign messages. By analyzing the preferences and sentiments of voters, politicians can tailor their communication strategies to appeal directly to individuals' political proclivities.

6.3. Challenges and Ethical Considerations

Despite its efficiency and effectiveness, the use of AI in voter profiling isn't without its challenges. The accuracy of predictions hinges largely on the quality and breadth of data. Incorrect or incomplete data can lead to flawed predictions, which in turn can impact election outcomes.

Furthermore, the ethics surrounding data collection and privacy remain a significant concern. Voter profiling has the potential to intrude on voters' privacy and may even be used unethically to manipulate public sentiment. Regulations and safeguards are necessary to prevent such misuse and to protect the personal information of voters.

Then, there's the issue of transparency. AI operates in a somewhat 'black box' manner, with many of its processes and decisions being opaque and incomprehensible to the layman. Greater transparency in AI processes is critical in reinforcing trust and ensuring ethically sound practices.

6.4. Gazing into the Future

Looking ahead, we can expect AI to continue playing a decisive role in voter profiling and, by extension, politics. With advancements in ML, NLP, and other AI technologies, the depth and accuracy of voter profiling are set to increase, enhancing the insights available to politicians and campaigners.

In conclusion, the application of AI in voter profiling is both an opportunity and a challenge. While it offers an efficient and precise way of understanding voters' sentiments and behaviors, it also creates ethical dilemmas that must be carefully managed. Only by navigating these complex issues can we fully harness AI's potential in reshaping politics.

Chapter 7. The Threat and Promise of AI in Political Propaganda

The digital era has redefined how political discourse unfolds. Among the myriad changes brought by technology, perhaps the most profound is how information - and, in turn, propaganda - is disseminated. Propaganda has been a part of politics since time immemorial. However, artificial intelligence(AI) has altered its landscape drastically. This transformation carries both threat and promise, which we'll delve into exhaustively.

7.1. The Evolution of Political Propaganda

As a first step, let's track propaganda's evolution. For centuries, propaganda was a high-effort, high-reach endeavor. With the advent of mass media – newspapers, radio, and TV – the reach expanded, but the effort remained high. Digital technology, specifically social media, changed the game by significantly reducing the difficulty of creating and distributing propaganda, while vastly expanding its reach.

A critical aspect of this evolution is the personalization and targeting facilitated by technology. Instead of broad demographic or geographical targets, propagandists can now craft and deliver messages at an individual level, based both on the recipient's digital profile and real-time online behavior. AI plays a fundamental part in this shift.

7.2. The Threat of AI in Political Propaganda

Understanding the threats posed by AI within political propaganda requires recognizing how AI leverages data to offer personalized content and how these personalized messages shape our political environment.

AI's threat lies in its ability to exploit human biases and emotions. By leveraging personal data, AI algorithms can target individuals with messages that reinforce existing beliefs or prey on fears. These messages, often called 'micro-target' propaganda, can be subtly introduced into the individual's information consumption, making its influence all the more insidious.

This capacity for manipulation poses significant risks to healthy political discourse. When AI-propelled propaganda reinforces extreme views or spreads disinformation, it polarizes societies and erodes shared realities, undermining informed deliberation - the bedrock of democratic systems. Examples of this threat include Russia's manipulation of social media in the 2016 U.S. Presidential Elections and the Cambridge Analytica scandal.

Moreover, AI can also produce deepfakes — hyper-realistic, manipulated videos that portray real people saying or doing things they did not. These deepfakes can be weaponized to distribute false information, sway opinions, or cause confusion and cynicism towards the political process.

7.3. The Promise of AI in Political Propaganda

Despite its threats, AI is not an inherently malevolent technology. In fact, AI has the potential to rectify some of the issues it also exacerbates. The following are notable opportunities that the integration of AI in political propaganda presents.

The same personalization that makes micro-target propaganda possible can also foster increased political engagement. Personalized messages, when used responsibly, can motivate citizens to participate in political processes by presenting relatable issues and understandable communications.

AI's analytical capabilities can decipher public sentiment accurately. When applied constructively, this ability can enhance policy decision-making, ensuring that it aligns better with the people's needs and aspirations.

Moreover, the development of AI-powered tools for detecting and countering fake news and disinformation is gathering pace. Google's Jigsaw, for instance, uses AI to spot and censor online hate speech and counter-terrorism propaganda.

7.4. Navigating the Dual Nature of AI in Political Propaganda

The countervailing threats and promises of AI in political propaganda indicate a duality that needs careful navigation. The role of AI in politics is not to replace human judgment - it should serve as a tool to work alongside human discretion, making processes smoother, transparent, and accountable.

Regulation has a critical role in this era of AI-propelled political communication. Governments must ensure the fair use of AI, promoting transparency and accountability in its application. They should also invest in digital literacy programs to equip citizens with the skills to discern valid information from propaganda.

Lastly, the ethics of AI systems should be a priority. Building AI systems with a core emphasis on fairness, transparency, and human dignity can go a long way towards minimizing the threats while maximizing the promises AI presents within political propaganda.

Indeed, the intersection of AI and political propaganda offers both risks and opportunities. Understanding and navigating these will be crucial to our digital democracy's health. We must remember, though, that AI doesn't drive our politics. We do. The technology is merely a reflection of our actions, aspirations, and indeed, our failures - reminding us to be the drivers, not the driven, in this influential AI era.

Chapter 8. Case Studies: Successful Employment of AI in Global Political Spectrum

In the last decade, AI has proven its capability in the political spectrum through various case studies globally. Analyzing data patterns, bolstering campaign strategies, and optimizing constituent services are just the tip of the iceberg of AI's impact in politics. We'll delve into a few key case studies that demonstrate the successful application of AI in politics.

8.1. Global Powers Leverage Predictive Analysis in Election Forecasting

One notable example of AI involvement in the political sphere was during the 2012 United States' Presidential Election. The campaign team of President Barack Obama leveraged AI in the form of predictive analysis to gain electoral benefits. Using data analytics, the Obama team was able to identify undecided citizens, predict their voting behavior, and target them with tailored messages. The application of AI resulted in a remarkable victory for President Obama.

Similarly, during the 2017 French Presidential Election, candidate Emmanuel Macron's campaign used AI for sentiment analysis by scanning the internet. Social media websites, blogs, forums, and newspaper comments sections were searched by AI's deep learning algorithms to understand the issues that people felt most strongly about and use this information to tailor their campaign messaging.

8.2. Social Media Manipulation by AI-Powered Bots

Social media has emerged as a powerful tool in politics - for engagement, PR and even propagating disinformation. During the United Kingdom's Brexit Referendum in 2016, the presence of AI-powered bots was significantly noticed influencing public opinion on social media. By spreading unsubstantiated news stories and arguments for 'Leave,' these AI bots played a role in swaying public sentiment.

Similarly, during the 2016 U.S. Presidential Elections, researchers have noted the extensive use of AI bots driving discourse on various platforms. Sharing information and engaging with human users, these bot accounts influenced public opinion and even claimed to have swayed the election's outcome.

8.3. Harnessing AI to Promote Transparency and Anti-Corruption Measures

In addition to election and campaign strategies, governments worldwide are using AI to improve governance. A prime example is the government of Singapore, which uses AI to forecast and prevent potential corruption cases in its public service sector. The AI system analyzes transaction patterns and raises red flags when irregularities are detected, thus promoting accountability and transparency.

AI is also being used to combat tax evasion in Brazil. The Carf (Administrative Council for Tax Appeals), part of Brazil's Ministry of Finance, uses AI to analyze legal suits, jurisprudence, and regulations to avoid misinterpretation or intentional manipulation of the law by taxpayers and agents.

8.4. AI for Disaster Management and Climate Change Mitigation

Artificial intelligence has played a pivotal role in disaster management as well. For instance, the Australian government has employed AI to predict bushfires. Hailed as 'AI4Wildfire,' the system uses satellite imagery to detect potential fire threats, helping to prevent calamity and aid in resource deployment.

AI is also aiding in climate change mitigation. The government of Finland has launched an AI-based solution to forecast energy consumption. The AI uses weather data to predict electricity demand, helping in the efficient allocation of renewable energy resources.

These cases highlight the successful employment of AI in the global political spectrum. With AI rapidly evolving, its potential to revolutionize politics and governance is immense, opening multiple avenues that could reshape societies. Therefore, understanding the implications of AI in politics is crucial, setting the tone for the future of governance and citizen engagement.

These examples are just a glimpse into the intersection of politics and AI. From election forecasting to improving public services, these instances highlight that the AI revolution isn't headed our way, it's already here. However, it's not without its challenges. In the next chapter, we will delve into potential threats and ethical considerations around integrating AI in the political landscape.

Chapter 9. Dissecting Failures: Lessons from Misuses of AI in Politics

There's an old saying that has been adapted to countless scenarios: "To err is human, to really foul things up requires a computer." With AI's increasing impact on politics, this age-old adage is becoming more applicable than ever. While AI has brought about unprecedented advances in election forecasting, campaign strategy, and governance, these achievements are not without failure.

9.1. The Cambridge Analytica Scandal: Data Misuse on a Grand Scale

In 2018, the sphere of AI and politics was rocked by a scandal of monumental proportions. Cambridge Analytica, a now-defunct British political consulting firm, wrongfully procured personal data from millions of Facebook users without their consent to build psychological profiles and target users with political advertising. This scandal highlighted the perilous risks associated with AI's capability to manipulate public opinion.

9.2. Failure in Election Forecasting: Underestimating the 'Trump Effect'

Another high-profile stumble in AI happened during the 2016 United States presidential race. Most election forecasting models that employed AI and machine learning confidently predicted a comfortable win for Hillary Clinton. However, the opposite happened. These models failed to account for unexpected aspects like the novelty of Trump's campaign and the muted, yet potent, sway of disillusioned voters. The failure underlines the potential dangers of over-reliance on AI and underscores the importance of infusing human intuition and understanding into AI models.

9.3. The Twitter Political Ad Ban: A Struggle to Balance Free Speech and Misinformation

In late 2019, Twitter announced its decision to ban political advertising on its platform to curb the spread of misinformation. This decision was met with opposition, as critics argued that it stifled free speech. The ramifications of this decision highlighted that AI solutions must carefully consider the social, political, and ethical implications of their use in politics.

9.4. Governance and Policy Failures: The PredPol Controversy

AI's impact on governance and policy-making was sharply brought into focus with the controversy surrounding the predictive policing tool PredPol. Advocates of the tool claimed it would make policing more efficient and objective by predicting potential crime hotspots. However, the tool faced severe backlash for perpetuating racial bias, thereby exacerbating systemic problems in policing. This failure underscores the need for a robust and transparent framework to guide the implementation and monitoring of AI in policy-making.

9.5. AI and Political Bots: The Battle Against Fake News

AI has been widely misused to propagate fake news, particularly through political bots that masquerade as humans on social media platforms, spreading disinformation and sowing discord. The 2016 elections witnessed an unprecedented deluge of such bots, clouding public discourse, and skewing perceptions. This misuse of AI once again spotlights the need for comprehensive legislation and digital literacy to combat online disinformation.

As we dissect these failures, several lessons emerge. The unchecked use of AI in politics can have grave societal implications, giving rise to sinister tactics like large-scale data misuse and the spread of fake news. AI applications must be guided by robust ethical frameworks that place human rights and privacy at their core. We must also remember that despite its advancing sophistication, AI is still an assistive tool and should complement, rather than replace, human judgment in political processes. Insulating AI applications from bias is another crucial task that policymakers, technologists, and civil society must together address.

Moreover, digitization must be complemented by digital literacy, equipping citizens to critically assess the information they consume online. Lastly, as with any technology, AI in politics will have its share of failures, serving as valuable lessons to drive iterative improvements. Stumbles, after all, pave the way for progress in this intriguing intersection of AI and politics.

Chapter 10. Emerging Trends and the Future of AI in Politics

Artificial Intelligence (AI) is an intricate web of adaptable software systems that can mimic certain aspects of human cognition. The powerful pull of AI has impacted varying sectors in our society, but its mark on politics may be less visible than expected. From political campaigns and elections to policy-making and governance, the influence of AI is fascinating and somewhat paradoxical.

10.1. Rise of AI-Infused Political Campaigns

One cannot embark a discussion on AI in politics without delving into the modern phenomenon of AI-driven political campaigns. There's a growing trend of harnessing big data sets and algorithmic analysis to refine campaign strategies, a method led by the predictive power of AI.

In the battlefield of public opinion, AI is a formidable ally. Machine learning models can analyze a wealth of data harvested from both online and offline sources. This data could range from basic demographic information to tweets, Facebook posts, or even online shopping behavior. By analyzing this vast array of data, AI systems can identify voting patterns, gauge public sentiment and even segment target audiences with granularity.

The AI algorithms used in these campaigns are designed to learn and adapt over time. They constantly refine the campaign's messaging and target demographics as more data streams in. This adaptive learning process can significantly improve campaigning, ensuring resources are efficiently allocated and campaign messages hit the mark.

10.2. Algorithms and Election Forecasting

Accurately forecasting an election's outcome is notoriously tricky. But the computational power and predictive algorithms of AI bring a certain degree of accuracy that is hard to rival. By distilling vast amounts of data, election forecasting is becoming more precise, a development that dramatically changes the dynamics of strategic campaigning.

Programming these AI systems involves a delicate balance. Traditional mathematical techniques are blended with machine learning, translating inputs into readable, understandable, and most importantly, accurate outputs. These systems consider various factors like historical voting patterns, current geopolitical conditions, and public sentiment, among others.

However, a fair caution - AI in election forecasting is not infallible. While these systems can predict outcomes with higher levels of precision than ever before, anomalies can still slip through. We only have to look to examples from the past, where sophisticated AI systems also claimed the impossibility of certain outcomes.

10.3. AI and Social Media: A Powerful Alliance

The relationship between social media and politics has grown increasingly important. That said, the advent of AI adds another layer of complexity and opportunity to this dynamic. Social media platforms, leveraged with AI, are capable of molding public opinion and political sentiment more than ever before.

When integrated with AI, social media enables an unprecedented level of granular demographic targeting. AI can painstakingly profile an individual's political affiliations, personal interests, group associations, and the likelihood of their turnout in voting. Such rich insights facilitate tailored, hyper-personalized campaign messages to specific demographics.

However, there's a downside. The shadow of 'fake news' and disinformation looms large. Experts warn that AI-generated fake content, or 'deepfakes', are capable of distorting truths and fostering misinformation. Hence, regulatory norms are essential to maintain ethical standards.

10.4. AI and Policy-making

The marriage of AI and policy-making can yield mutual benefits. On one hand, AI can help in structuring public policy decisions by quantitatively analyzing various policy options and their likely impacts. AI can process large amounts of data, model complex systems, and predict future trends, proving invaluable to the policy-making process.

On the flip side, the policies can shape the direction in which AI evolves. Regulations related to data privacy, AI ethics, and industrial applications of AI can determine how businesses, governments, and individuals interact with this technology.

10.5. Future of AI in Politics - A Conclusion

Understanding and acknowledging the profound role of AI in politics is essential as its influence is only set to grow. As the technology matures, it will continue to transform and redefine the political landscape. We will witness more nuanced uses of AI in campaigning, policymaking, and governance. However, with these prospects come significant challenges. Issues like bias in AI, data privacy, and the problems of 'deepfakes' will require careful attention and strong regulations.

In sum, AI in politics is a brave new world. It's described best as a double-edged sword – it promises significant benefits if used well, but it can be harmful if misused or allowed to run unchecked. Recognizing this, there's an urgent need for political leaders, technology experts, and citizens to work together, to harness the potential of AI in a responsible, ethical manner that equally respects privacy rights and democratic principles.

By understanding the intricacies and implications of AI, we hope to push forward a future where technology serves to further democratic processes, rather than hinder them.

Chapter 11. Making the Most of AI in Politics: Recommendations for Stakeholders

The invisible yet profound influence of artificial intelligence (AI) has the potential to reshape the political landscape in unprecedented ways. As we become more reliant on these technologies, it's crucial for key political stakeholders and decision-makers to navigate this vast, often perplexing field effectively. This chapter offer insights and provides recommendations to harness the power of AI for optimized political processes.

11.1. Understanding AI and Politics

Artificial Intelligence (AI) encompasses a broad spectrum of technologies which, to varying degrees, can mimic or even outperform human intelligence in specific tasks. From search engines to self-driving cars, AI technologies have pervaded practically every area of our lives. Importantly, the power of AI extends to politics too.

Politics, from policy-making to elections, requires intricate decision-making and intricate communication strategies. AI, with its ability to process and analyze vast amounts of data, can help make these processes more effective and efficient. Yet, it can also pose ethical challenges, such as issues related to privacy, transparency, and the digital divide.

Critically examining the overlap of AI and politics, considering both its promises and potential problems, is key for politicians, strategists, activists, technologists, and citizens alike. The first step? Understand the capabilities and limitations of AI in the political realm.

11.2. Leveraging AI in Campaigning

One of the predominant areas where AI's influence is both evident and powerful is in political campaigning. AI platforms can process enormous amounts of data - from social media posts to voting records – to identify key voter segments and tailor persuasive messages for them. Candidate promotion, fundraising, opposition research, voter turnout - nearly all aspects of campaigning can be optimized with the use of AI.

Recommendation #1: **Adopt AI technologies** for intricate data analysis to understand public sentiment and tailor campaign strategies accordingly.

Recommendation #2: **Ensure responsible AI usage** to keep trust with constituents. Maintaining transparency and prioritizing data privacy can prevent technology-powered campaign strategies from backfiring.

11.3. Engine of Policy-Making

AI can enable politicians to make well-informed decisions by providing insights hidden in large sets of complex data. Moreover, AI models can simulate the impacts of policies, helping policymakers anticipate potential outcomes and consequences.

Recommendation #3: **Deploy AI in policy analysis and projection.** Using AI to predict policy outcomes can lead to more strategic decision-making and, ultimately, more effective policies.

11.4. Ensuring an Equal Playing Field

While the opportunities of using AI in politics are considerable, so too are the challenges and threats. Notably, the use of AI can exacerbate the existing digital divide, particularly for under-represented communities. It's critical that access to, benefits from, and influence over AI is evenly and fairly distributed.

Recommendation #4: **Promote AI literacy.** Understandably, AI in politics can be a convoluted topic for many citizens. Therefore, it's essential to build robust education programs to improve AI literacy across the populace.

Recommendation #5: **Ensure tech equity.** To avoid further deepening the digital divide, policies should be implemented to ensure equal access to AI technologies. It's pivotal to enable all communities to leverage AI opportunities.

11.5. AI Policy and Regulation

The potent potential of AI to drive change in political landscapes can be both positive and negative. It is essential, therefore, for governments to establish policies and regulations that foster fairness, privacy, security, transparency, and accountability.

Recommendation #6: **Develop comprehensive AI legislation.** As our reliance on AI grows and complexities increase, it's vital for governments to establish clear and comprehensive legislation to govern AI usage.

Recommendation #7: **Encourage multi-stakeholder participation.** Including tech companies, politicians, and citizens in policy development can help ensure diverse voices are heard, and resultant policies are balanced and equitable.

The conjunction of AI and politics is a reality of our contemporary world. Grasping its intricacies and harnessing its power can equip political stakeholders with a significant advantage. However, let's not forget - while AI has a transformative potential, it's merely a tool. The human judgment, values, intellect, and empathy at its helm retain unparalleled importance.

www.ingramcontent.com/pod-product-compliance
Lightning Source LLC
Chambersburg PA
CBHW071040260726
48661CB00007B/3090